SONGS OF
KABIR

Translated by
RABINDRANATH TAGORE

Assisted by
EVELYN UNDERHILL

DOVER PUBLICATIONS, INC.
Mineola, New York

Bibliographical Note

This Dover edition, first published in 2004, is an unabridged republication of the work originally published by The India Society, London, in 1914 under the title *One Hundred Poems of Kabir.*

Library of Congress Cataloging-in-Publication Data

Kabir, 15th cent.
  [Songs. English. Selections]
  Songs of Kabir / Kabir ; translated by Rabindranath Tagore ; assisted by Evelyn Underhill.—Dover ed.
      p. cm.
  "Based upon the printed Hindi text with Bengali translation of Mr. Kshiti Mohan Sen."—Introd., 1914 ed.
  Originally published: One hundred poems of Kabir. London: The India Society, 1914.
  ISBN-13: 978-0-486-43358-5
  ISBN-10: 0-486-43358-7
  I. Tagore, Rabindranath, 1861–1941. II. Underhill, Evelyn, 1875–1941.
III. Title.

PK2095.K3A25 2004
891.4'312—dc22

2003063501

Manufactured in the United States by RR Donnelley
43358704   2016
www.doverpublications.com

INTRODUCTION

THE poet Kabīr, a selection from whose songs is here for the first time offered to English readers, is one of the most interesting personalities in the history of Indian mysticism. Born in or near Benares, of Mohammedan parents, and probably about the year 1440, he became in early life a disciple of the celebrated Hindu ascetic Rāmānanda. Rāmānanda had brought to Northern India the religious revival which Rāmānuja, the great twelfth-century reformer of Brāhmanism, had initiated in the South. This revival was in part a reaction against the increasing formalism of the orthodox cult, in part an assertion of the demands of the heart as against the intense intellectualism of the Vedānta philosophy, the exaggerated monism which that philosophy proclaimed. It took in Rāmānuja's preaching the form of an ardent personal devotion to the God Vishnu, as representing the personal aspect of the Divine Nature: that mystical "religion of love" which everywhere makes its appearance at a certain level of spiritual culture, and which creeds and philosophies are powerless to kill.

Though such a devotion is indigenous in Hinduism, and finds expression in many passages of the Bhagavad Gītā, there was in its mediæval revival a large element of syncretism. Rāmānanda, through whom its spirit is said to have reached Kabīr, appears to have been a man of wide religious culture, and full of missionary enthusiasm. Living at the moment in which the impassioned poetry and deep philosophy of the great Persian mystics, Attār, Sādī, Jalālu'ddīn Rūmī, and Hāfiz, were exercising a powerful influence on the religious thought of India, he dreamed of reconciling this intense and personal Mohammedan mysticism with the traditional theology of Brāhmanism. Some have regarded both these great religious leaders as influenced also by Christian thought and life: but as this is a point upon which competent authorities hold widely divergent views, its discussion is not attempted here. We may safely assert, however, that in their teachings, two—perhaps three—apparently antagonistic streams of intense spiritual culture met, as Jewish and Hellenistic thought met in the early Christian Church: and it is one of the outstanding characteristics of Kabīr's genius that he was able in his poems to fuse them into one.

A great religious reformer, the founder of a sect to which nearly a million northern Hindus still belong, it is yet supremely as a mystical poet that Kabīr lives for us. His fate has been that of many

revealers of Reality. A hater of religious exclu-
sivism, and seeking above all things to initiate men
into the liberty of the children of God, his followers
have honoured his memory by re-erecting in a new
place the barriers which he laboured to cast down.
But his wonderful songs survive, the spontaneous
expressions of his vision and his love; and it is by
these, not by the didactic teachings associated with
his name, that he makes his immortal appeal to the
heart. In these poems a wide range of mystical
emotion is brought into play: from the loftiest
abstractions, the most other-worldly passion for
the Infinite, to the most intimate and personal
realization of God, expressed in homely metaphors
and religious symbols drawn indifferently from
Hindu and Mohammedan belief. It is impossible
to say of their author that he was Brāhman or
Sūfī, Vedāntist or Vaishnavite. He is, as he
says himself, "at once the child of Allah and of
Rām." That Supreme Spirit Whom he knew and
adored, and to Whose joyous friendship he sought
to induct the souls of other men, transcended
whilst He included all metaphysical categories, all
credal definitions; yet each contributed something
to the description of that Infinite and Simple
Totality Who revealed Himself, according to their
measure, to the faithful lovers of all creeds.

Kabīr's story is surrounded by contradictory
legends, on none of which reliance can be placed.
Some of these emanate from a Hindu, some from

a Mohammedan source, and claim him by turns as a Sūfī and a Brāhman saint. His name, however, is practically a conclusive proof of Moslem ancestry: and the most probable tale is that which represents him as the actual or adopted child of a Mohammedan weaver of Benares, the city in which the chief events of his life took place.

In fifteenth-century Benares the syncretistic tendencies of Bhakti religion had reached full development. Sūfīs and Brāhmans appear to have met in disputation: the most spiritual members of both creeds frequenting the teachings of Rāmānanda, whose reputation was then at its height. The boy Kabīr, in whom the religious passion was innate, saw in Rāmānanda his destined teacher; but knew how slight were the chances that a Hindu guru would accept a Mohammedan as disciple. He therefore hid upon the steps of the river Ganges, where Rāmānanda was accustomed to bathe; with the result that the master, coming down to the water, trod upon his body unexpectedly, and exclaimed in his astonishment, "Rām! Rām!"—the name of the incarnation under which he worshipped God. Kabīr then declared that he had received the mantra of initiation from Rāmānanda's lips, and was by it admitted to discipleship. In spite of the protests of orthodox Brāhmans and Mohammedans, both equally annoyed by this contempt of theological landmarks, he persisted in his claim; thus exhibit-

ing in action that very principle of religious syn-
thesis which Rāmānanda had sought to establish
in thought. Rāmānanda appears to have accepted
him, and though Mohammedan legends speak of
the famous Sūfī Pīr, Takkī of Jhansī, as Kabīr's
master in later life, the Hindu saint is the only
human teacher to whom in his songs he acknow-
ledges indebtedness.

The little that we know of Kabīr's life contra-
dicts many current ideas concerning the Oriental
mystic. Of the stages of discipline through which
he passed, the manner in which his spiritual genius
developed, we are completely ignorant. He seems
to have remained for years the disciple of Rāmā-
nanda, joining in the theological and philosophical
arguments which his master held with all the great
Mullahs and Brāhmans of his day; and to this
source we may perhaps trace his acquaintance
with the terms of Hindu and Sūfī philosophy. He
may or may not have submitted to the traditional
education of the Hindu or the Sūfī contemplative:
it is clear, at any rate, that he never adopted the
life of the professional ascetic, or retired from the
world in order to devote himself to bodily morti-
fications and the exclusive pursuit of the contem-
plative life. Side by side with his interior life of
adoration, its artistic expression in music and words
—for he was a skilled musician as well as a poet—
he lived the sane and diligent life of the Oriental
craftsman. All the legends agree on this point:

that Kabīr was a weaver, a simple and unlettered man, who earned his living at the loom. Like Paul the tentmaker, Boehme the cobbler, Bunyan the tinker, Tersteegen the ribbon-maker, he knew how to combine vision and industry; the work of his hands helped rather than hindered the impassioned meditation of his heart. Hating mere bodily austerities, he was no ascetic, but a married man, the father of a family—a circumstance which Hindu legends of the monastic type vainly attempt to conceal or explain—and it was from out of the heart of the common life that he sang his rapturous lyrics of divine love. Here his works corroborate the traditional story of his life. Again and again he extols the life of home, the value and reality of diurnal existence, with its opportunities for love and renunciation; pouring contempt upon the professional sanctity of the Yogi, who "has a great beard and matted locks, and looks like a goat," and on all who think it necessary to flee a world pervaded by love, joy, and beauty—the proper theatre of man's quest—in order to find that One Reality Who has "spread His form of love throughout all the world."[1]

It does not need much experience of ascetic literature to recognize the boldness and originality of this attitude in such a time and place. From the point of view of orthodox sanctity, whether Hindu or Mohammedan, Kabīr was plainly a

[1] Cf. Poems Nos. XXI, XL, XLIII, LXVI, LXXVI.

heretic; and his frank dislike of all institutional religion, all external observance—which was as thorough and as intense as that of the Quakers themselves—completed, so far as ecclesiastical opinion was concerned, his reputation as a dangerous man. The "simple union" with Divine Reality which he perpetually extolled, as alike the duty and the joy of every soul, was independent both of ritual and of bodily austerities; the God whom he proclaimed was "neither in Kaaba nor in Kailāsh." Those who sought Him needed not to go far; for He awaited discovery everywhere, more accessible to "the washerwoman and the carpenter" than to the self-righteous holy man.[1] Therefore the whole apparatus of piety, Hindu and Moslem alike—the temple and mosque, idol and holy water, scriptures and priests—were denounced by this inconveniently clear-sighted poet as mere substitutes for reality; dead things intervening between the soul and its love—

The images are all lifeless, they cannot speak: I know, for I have cried aloud to them.
The Purāna and the Korān are mere words: lifting up the curtain, I have seen.[2]

This sort of thing cannot be tolerated by any organized church; and it is not surprising that Kabīr, having his head-quarters in Benares, the very centre of priestly influence, was subjected to considerable persecution. The well-known legend

[1] Poems I, II, XLI.   [2] Poems XLII, LXV, LXVII.

of the beautiful courtesan sent by the Brāhmans to tempt his virtue, and converted, like the Magdalen, by her sudden encounter with the initiate of a higher love, preserves the memory of the fear and dislike with which he was regarded by the ecclesiastical powers. Once at least, after the performance of a supposed miracle of healing, he was brought before the Emperor Sikandar Lodī, and charged with claiming the possession of divine powers. But Sikandar Lodī, a ruler of considerable culture, was tolerant of the eccentricities of saintly persons belonging to his own faith. Kabīr, being of Mohammedan birth, was outside the authority of the Brāhmans, and technically classed with the Sūfīs, to whom great theological latitude was allowed. Therefore, though he was banished in the interests of peace from Benares, his life was spared. This seems to have happened in 1495, when he was nearly sixty years of age; it is the last event in his career of which we have definite knowledge. Thenceforth he appears to have moved about amongst various cities of northern India, the centre of a group of disciples; continuing in exile that life of apostle and poet of love to which, as he declares in one of his songs, he was destined "from the beginning of time." In 1518, an old man, broken in health, and with hands so feeble that he could no longer make the music which he loved, he died at Maghar near Gorakhpur.

A beautiful legend tells us that after his death

his Mohammedan and Hindu disciples disputed
the possession of his body; which the Mohamme-
dans wished to bury, the Hindus to burn. As they
argued together, Kabīr appeared before them, and
told them to lift the shroud and look at that which
lay beneath. They did so, and found in the place of
the corpse a heap of flowers; half of which were
buried by the Mohammedans at Maghar, and half
carried by the Hindus to the holy city of Benares
to be burned—fitting conclusion to a life which
had made fragrant the most beautiful doctrines of
two great creeds.

II

The poetry of mysticism might be defined on
the one hand as a temperamental reaction to the
vision of Reality: on the other, as a form of
prophecy. As it is the special vocation of the
mystical consciousness to mediate between two
orders, going out in loving adoration towards God
and coming home to tell the secrets of Eternity to
other men; so the artistic self-expression of this
consciousness has also a double character. It is
love-poetry, but love-poetry which is often written
with a missionary intention.

Kabīr's songs are of this kind: outbirths at once
of rapture and of charity. Written in the popular
Hindī, not in the literary tongue, they were de-
liberately addressed—like the vernacular poetry
of Jacopone da Todì and Richard Rolle—to the

people rather than to the professionally religious class; and all must be struck by the constant employment in them of imagery drawn from the common life, the universal experience. It is by the simplest metaphors, by constant appeals to needs, passions, relations which all men understand—the bridegroom and bride, the guru and disciple, the pilgrim, the farmer, the migrant bird—that he drives home his intense conviction of the reality of the soul's intercourse with the Transcendent. There are in his universe no fences between the "natural" and "supernatural" worlds; everything is a part of the creative Play of God, and therefore —even in its humblest details—capable of revealing the Player's mind.

This willing acceptance of the here-and-now as a means of representing supernal realities is a trait common to the greatest mystics. For them, when they have achieved at last the true theopathetic state, all aspects of the universe possess equal authority as sacramental declarations of the Presence of God; and their fearless employment of homely and physical symbols—often startling and even revolting to the unaccustomed taste—is in direct proportion to the exaltation of their spiritual life. The works of the great Sūfīs, and amongst the Christians of Jacopone da Todì, Ruysbroeck, Boehme, abound in illustrations of this law. Therefore we must not be surprised to find in Kabīr's songs—his desperate attempts to communicate

his ecstasy and persuade other men to share it—
a constant juxtaposition of concrete and meta-
physical language; swift alternations between the
most intensely anthropomorphic, the most subtly
philosophical, ways of apprehending man's com-
munion with the Divine. The need for this alter-
nation, and its entire naturalness for the mind which
employs it, is rooted in his concept, or vision, of
the Nature of God; and unless we make some
attempt to grasp this, we shall not go far in our
understanding of his poems.

Kabīr belongs to that small group of supreme
mystics—amongst whom St. Augustine, Ruys-
broeck, and the Sūfī poet Jalālu'ddīn Rūmī are
perhaps the chief—who have achieved that which
we might call the synthetic vision of God. These
have resolved the perpetual opposition between
the personal and impersonal, the transcendent
and immanent, static and dynamic aspects of the
Divine Nature; between the Absolute of philo-
sophy and the "sure true Friend" of devotional
religion. They have done this, not by taking these
apparently incompatible concepts one after the
other; but by ascending to a height of spiritual
intuition at which they are, as Ruysbroeck said,
"melted and merged in the Unity," and perceived
as the completing opposites of a perfect Whole.
This proceeding entails for them—and both Kabīr
and Ruysbroeck expressly acknowledge it—a uni-
verse of three orders: Becoming, Being, and that

which is "More than Being," *i.e.*, God.[1] God is
here felt to be not the final abstraction, but the
one actuality. He inspires, supports, indeed in-
habits, both the durational, conditioned, finite world
of Becoming and the unconditioned, non-succes-
sional, infinite world of Being; yet utterly tran-
scends them both. He is the omnipresent Reality,
the "All-pervading" within Whom "the worlds are
being told like beads." In His personal aspect He
is the "beloved Fakīr," teaching and companioning
each soul. Considered as Immanent Spirit, He is
"the Mind within the mind." But all these are at
best partial aspects of His nature, mutually correc-
tive: as the Persons in the Christian doctrine of
the Trinity—to which this theological diagram
bears a striking resemblance—represent different
and compensating experiences of the Divine Unity
within which they are resumed. As Ruysbroeck
discerned a plane of reality upon which "we can
speak no more of Father, Son, and Holy Spirit,
but only of One Being, the very substance of the
Divine Persons"; so Kabīr says that "beyond
both the limited *and* the limitless is He, the Pure
Being."[2]

Brahma, then, is the Ineffable Fact compared
with which "the distinction of the Conditioned
from the Unconditioned is but a word": at once
the utterly transcendent One of Absolutist philo-
sophy, and the personal Lover of the individual

---

[1] Nos. VII and XLIX.   [2] No. VII.

soul—"common to all and special to each," as one
Christian mystic has it. The need felt by Kabīr
for both these ways of describing Reality is a proof
of the richness and balance of his spiritual experi-
ence; which neither cosmic nor anthropomorphic
symbols, taken alone, could express. More absolute
than the Absolute, more personal than the human
mind, Brahma therefore exceeds whilst He in-
cludes all the concepts of philosophy, all the
passionate intuitions of the heart. He is the Great
Affirmation, the fount of energy, the source of life
and love, the unique satisfaction of desire. His
creative word is the *Om* or "Everlasting Yea."
The negative philosophy, which strips from the
Divine Nature all Its attributes and—defining
Him only by that which He is not—reduces Him
to an "Emptiness," is abhorrent to this most vital
of poets. Brahma, he says, "may never be found
in abstractions." He is the One Love who per-
vades the world, discerned in His fullness only by
the eyes of love; and those who know Him thus
share, though they may never tell, the joyous and
ineffable secret of the universe.[1]

Now Kabīr, achieving this synthesis between
the personal and cosmic aspects of the Divine
Nature, eludes the three great dangers which
threaten mystical religion.

First, he escapes the excessive emotionalism,
the tendency to an exclusively anthropomorphic

[1] Nos. VII, XXVI, LXXVI, XC.

devotion, which results from an unrestricted cult of Divine Personality, especially under an incarnational form; seen in India in the exaggerations of Krishna worship, in Europe in the sentimental extravagances of certain Christian saints.

Next, he is protected from the soul-destroying conclusions of pure monism, inevitable if its logical implications are pressed home: that is, the identity of substance between God and the soul, with its corollary of the total absorption of that soul in the Being of God as the goal of the spiritual life. For the thorough-going monist the soul, in so far as it is real, is substantially identical with God; and the true object of existence is the making patent of this latent identity, the realization which finds expression in the Vedāntist formula "That art thou." But Kabīr says that Brahma and the creature are " ever distinct, yet ever united"; that the wise man knows the spiritual as well as the material world to "be no more than His footstool."¹ The soul's union with Him is a love union, a mutual inhabitation; that essentially dualistic relation which all mystical religion expresses, not a self-mergence which leaves no place for personality. This eternal distinction, the mysterious union-in-separateness of God and the soul, is a necessary doctrine of all sane mysticism; for no scheme which fails to find a place for it can represent more than a fragment of that soul's intercourse with the spiritual world. Its affirmation

¹ Nos. VII and IX.

was one of the distinguishing features of the
Vaishnavite reformation preached by Rāmānuja;
the principle of which had descended through
Rāmānanda to Kabīr.

Last, the warmly human and direct appre-
hension of God as the supreme Object of love, the
soul's comrade, teacher, and bridegroom, which is
so passionately and frequently expressed in Kabīr's
poems, balances and controls those abstract tend-
encies which are inherent in the metaphysical side
of his vision of Reality: and prevents it from de-
generating into that sterile worship of intellectual
formulae which became the curse of the Vedāntist
school. For the mere intellectualist, as for the
mere pietist, he has little approbation.[1] Love is
throughout his "absolute sole Lord": the unique
source of the more abundant life which he enjoys,
and the common factor which unites the finite and
infinite worlds. All is soaked in love: that love
which he described in almost Johannine language as
the "Form of God." The whole of creation is the
Play of the Eternal Lover; the living, changing,
growing expression of Brahma's love and joy. As
these twin passions preside over the generation of
human life, so "beyond the mists of pleasure and
pain" Kabīr finds them governing the creative acts
of God. His manifestation is love; His activity is
joy. Creation springs from one glad act of affirma-
tion: the Everlasting Yea, perpetually uttered with-

[1] Cf. especially Nos. LIX, LXVII, LXXV, XC, XCI.

in the depths of the Divine Nature.[1] In accordance with this concept of the universe as a Love-Game which eternally goes forward, a progressive manifestation of Brahma—one of the many notions which he adopted from the common stock of Hindu religious ideas, and illuminated by his poetic genius —movement, rhythm, perpetual change, forms an integral part of Kabīr's vision of Reality. Though the Eternal and Absolute is ever present to his consciousness, yet his concept of the Divine Nature is essentially dynamic. It is by the symbols of motion that he most often tries to convey it to us: as in his constant reference to dancing, or the strangely modern picture of that Eternal Swing of the Universe which is "held by the cords of love."[2]

It is a marked characteristic of mystical literature that the great contemplatives, in their effort to convey to us the nature of their communion with the supersensuous, are inevitably driven to employ some form of sensuous imagery: coarse and inaccurate as they know such imagery to be, even at the best. Our normal human consciousness is so completely committed to dependence on the senses, that the fruits of intuition itself are instinctively referred to them. In that intuition it seems to the mystics that all the dim cravings and partial apprehensions of sense find perfect fulfilment. Hence their constant declaration that they *see* the uncreated

[1] Nos. XVII, XXVI, LXXVI, LXXXII.   [2] No. XVI.

light, they *hear* the celestial melody, they *taste* the sweetness of the Lord, they know an ineffable fragrance, they feel the very contact of love. "Him verily seeing and fully feeling, Him spiritually hearing and Him delectably smelling and sweetly swallowing," as Julian of Norwich has it. In those amongst them who develop psycho-sensorial automatisms these parallels between sense and spirit may present themselves to consciousness in the form of hallucinations: as the light seen by Suso, the music heard by Rolle, the celestial perfumes which filled St. Catherine of Siena's cell, the physical wounds felt by St. Francis and St. Teresa. These are excessive dramatizations of the symbolism under which the mystic tends instinctively to represent his spiritual intuition to the surface consciousness. Here, in the special sense-perception which he feels to be most expressive of Reality, his peculiar idiosyncrasies come out.

Now Kabīr, as we might expect in one whose reactions to the spiritual order were so wide and various, uses by turn all the symbols of sense. He tells us that he has " seen without sight " the effulgence of Brahma, tasted the divine nectar, felt the ecstatic contact of Reality, smelt the fragrance of the heavenly flowers. But he was essentially a poet and musician: rhythm and harmony were to him the garments of beauty and truth. Hence in his lyrics he shows himself to be, like Richard Rolle, above all things a musical mystic. Creation, he says again

and again, is full of music: it *is* music. At the
heart of the Universe "white music is blossoming":
love weaves the melody, whilst renunciation beats
the time. It can be heard in the home as well as
in the heavens; discerned by the ears of common
men as well as by the trained senses of the ascetic.
Moreover, the body of every man is a lyre on
which Brahma, "the source of all music," plays.
Everywhere Kabīr discerns the " Unstruck Music
of the Infinite "—that celestial melody which the
angel played to St. Francis, that ghostly symphony
which filled the soul of Rolle with ecstatic joy.[1]
The one figure which he adopts from the Hindu
Pantheon and constantly uses, is that of Krishna
the Divine Flute Player.[2] He sees the supernal
music, too, in its visual embodiment, as rhythmical
movement: that mysterious dance of the universe
before the face of Brahma, which is at once an act
of worship and an expression of the infinite rap-
ture of the Immanent God.[3]

Yet in this wide and rapturous vision of the
universe Kabīr never loses touch with diurnal
existence, never forgets the common life. His feet
are firmly planted upon earth; his lofty and pas-
sionate apprehensions are perpetually controlled
by the activity of a sane and vigorous intellect, by
the alert commonsense so often found in persons

---

[1] Nos. XVII, XVIII, XXXIX, XLI, LIV, LXXVI,
LXXXIII, LXXXIX, XCVII.
[2] Nos. L, LIII, LXVIII.   [3] Nos. XXVI, XXXII, LXXVI.

of real mystical genius. The constant insistence on simplicity and directness, the hatred of all abstractions and philosophizings,[1] the ruthless criticism of external religion: these are amongst his most marked characteristics. God is the Root whence all manifestations, "material" and "spiritual," alike proceed; and God is the only need of man—"happiness shall be yours when you come to the Root."[2] Hence to those who keep their eye on the "one thing needful," denominations, creeds, ceremonies, the conclusions of philosophy, the disciplines of asceticism, are matters of comparative indifference. They represent merely the different angles from which the soul may approach that simple union with Brahma which is its goal; and are useful only in so far as they contribute to this consummation. So thorough-going is Kabīr's eclecticism, that he seems by turns Vedāntist and Vaishnavite, Pantheist and Transcendentalist, Brāhman and Sūfī. In the effort to tell the truth about that ineffable apprehension, so vast and yet so near, which controls his life, he seizes and twines together—as he might have woven together contrasting threads upon his loom—symbols and ideas drawn from the most violent and conflicting philosophies and faiths. All are needed, if he is ever to suggest the character of that One whom the Upanishad called "the Sun-coloured Being who is beyond this Darkness": as all the

---

[1] Nos. LXXV, LXXVIII, LXXX, XC.   [2] No. LXXX.

colours of the spectrum are needed if we would
demonstrate the simple richness of white light.
In thus adapting traditional materials to his own
use he follows a method common amongst the
mystics; who seldom exhibit any special love for
originality of form. They will pour their wine
into almost any vessel that comes to hand: gener-
ally using by preference—and lifting to new levels
of beauty and significance—the religious or philo-
sophic formulae current in their own day. Thus
we find that some of Kabīr's finest poems have
as their subjects the commonplaces of Hindu
philosophy and religion: the Līlā, or Sport, of God,
the Ocean of Bliss, the Bird of the Soul, Māyā,
the Hundred-petalled Lotus, and the " Formless
Form." Many, again, are soaked in Sūfī imagery
and feeling. Others use as their material the
ordinary surroundings and incidents of Indian life:
the temple bells, the ceremony of the lamps,
marriage, suttee, pilgrimage, the characters of the
seasons; all felt by him in their mystical aspect,
as sacraments of the soul's relation with Brahma.
In many of these a particularly beautiful and in-
timate feeling for Nature is shown.[1]

In the collection of songs here translated there
will be found examples which illustrate nearly every
aspect of Kabīr's thought, and all the fluctuations
of the mystic's emotion: the ecstasy, the despair,
the still beatitude, the eager self-devotion, the

[1] Nos. XV, XXIII, LXVII, LXXXVII, XCVIII.

flashes of wide illumination, the moments of inti-
mate love.   His wide and deep vision of the uni-
verse, the "Eternal Sport" of creation (LXXXII),
the worlds being "told like beads" within the Being
of God (XIV, XVI, XVII, LXXVI), is here seen
balanced by his lovely and delicate sense of inti-
mate communion with the Divine Friend, Lover,
Teacher of the soul (X, XI, XXIII, XXXV,
LI, LXXXV, LXXXVI, LXXXVIII, XCII,
XCIII; above all, the beautiful poem XXXIV). As
these apparently paradoxical views of Reality are
resolved in Brahma, so all other opposites are re-
conciled in Him: bondage and liberty, love and
renunciation, pleasure and pain (XVII, XXV, XL,
LXXXIX).   Union with Him is the one thing
that matters to the soul, its destiny and its need
(LI, LII, LIV, LXX, LXXIV, XCIII, XCVI);
and this union, this discovery of God, is the simplest
and most natural of all things, if we would but
grasp it (XLI, XLVI, LVI, LXXII, LXXVI,
LXXVIII, XCVII).   The union, however, is
brought about by love, not by knowledge or
ceremonial observances (XXXVIII, LIV, LV,
LIX, XCI); and the apprehension which that
union confers is ineffable—"neither This nor That,"
as Ruysbroeck has it (IX, XLVI, LXXVI). Real
worship and communion is in Spirit and in Truth
(XL, XLI, LVI, LXIII, LXV, LXX), therefore
idolatry is an insult to the Divine Lover (XLII,
LXIX) and the devices of professional sanctity

are useless apart from charity and purity of soul
(LIV, LXV, LXVI). Since all things, and
especially the heart of man, are God-inhabited,
God-possessed (XXVI, LVI, LXXVI, LXXXIX,
XCVII), He may best be found in the here-and-
now : in the normal, human, bodily existence, the
"mud" of material life (III, IV, VI, XXI, XXXIX,
XL, XLIII, XLVIII, LXXII). "We can reach
the goal without crossing the road" (LXXVI)—
not the cloister but the home is the proper theatre
of man's efforts : and if he cannot find God there,
he need not hope for success by going farther afield.
"In the home is reality." There love and detach-
ment, bondage and freedom, joy and pain play
by turns upon the soul; and it is from their conflict
that the Unstruck Music of the Infinite proceeds.
"Kabīr says: None but Brahma can evoke its
melodies."

III

This version of Kabīr's songs is chiefly the work
of Mr. Rabīndranāth Tagore, the trend of whose
mystical genius makes him—as all who read these
poems will see—a peculiarly sympathetic inter-
preter of Kabīr's vision and thought. It has been
based upon the printed Hindī text with Bengali
translation of Mr. Kshiti Mohan Sen; who has
gathered from many sources—sometimes from
books and manuscripts, sometimes from the lips of
wandering ascetics and minstrels—a large collec-

tion of poems and hymns to which Kabīr's name is attached, and carefully sifted the authentic songs from the many spurious works now attributed to him. These painstaking labours alone have made the present undertaking possible.

We have also had before us a manuscript English translation of 116 songs made by Mr. Ajit Kumār Chakravarty from Mr. Kshiti Mohan Sen's text, and a prose essay upon Kabīr from the same hand. From these we have derived great assistance. A considerable number of readings from the translation have been adopted by us; whilst several of the facts mentioned in the essay have been incorporated into this introduction. Our most grateful thanks are due to Mr. Ajit Kumār Chakravarty for the extremely generous and unselfish manner in which he has placed his work at our disposal.

E.U.

The reference of the headlines of the poems is to:

Śāntiniketana; Kabīr by Śrī Kshitimohan Sen, 4 parts, Brahmacharyāśrama, Bolpur, 1910-11.

For some assistance in normalizing the transliteration we are indebted to Prof. J. F. Blumhardt.

SONGS OF KABIR

I

I. 13. *mo ko kahāṇ ḍhūnṛo bande*

O SERVANT, where dost thou seek Me?
Lo! I am beside thee.
I am neither in temple nor in mosque: I am neither
in Kaaba nor in Kailash:
Neither am I in rites and ceremonies, nor in Yoga
and renunciation.
If thou art a true seeker, thou shalt at once see
Me: thou shalt meet Me in a moment of
time.
Kabir says, "O Sadhu! God is the breath of all
breath."

II

I. 16. *santan jāt na pūcho nirguṇiyāṇ*

IT is needless to ask of a saint the caste to
which he belongs;
For the priest, the warrior, the tradesman, and all
the thirty-six castes, alike are seeking for
God.

It is but folly to ask what the caste of a saint may
be;
The barber has sought God, the washer-woman,
and the carpenter—
Even Raidas was a seeker after God.
The Rishi Swapacha was a tanner by caste.
Hindus and Moslems alike have achieved that
End, where remains no mark of distinction.

III

I. 57.   sādho bhāī, jīvat hī karo āśā

O FRIEND! hope for Him whilst you live,
know whilst you live, understand whilst
you live: for in life deliverance abides.
If your bonds be not broken whilst living, what
hope of deliverance in death?
It is but an empty dream, that the soul shall have
union with Him because it has passed from
the body:
If He is found now, He is found then,
If not, we do but go to dwell in the City of Death.
If you have union now, you shall have it hereafter.
Bathe in the truth, know the true Guru, have faith
in the true Name!
Kabir says: "It is the Spirit of the quest which
helps; I am the slave of this Spirit of the
quest."

IV

I. 58. bāgo nā jā re nā jā

DO not go to the garden of flowers!
  O Friend! go not there;
In your body is the garden of flowers.
Take your seat on the thousand petals of the lotus,
  and there gaze on the Infinite Beauty.

V

I. 63. avadhū, māyā tajī na jāy

TELL me, Brother, how can I renounce
  Maya?
When I gave up the tying of ribbons, still I tied
  my garment about me:
When I gave up tying my garment, still I covered
  my body in its folds.
So, when I give up passion, I see that anger
  remains;
And when I renounce anger, greed is with me
  still;
And when greed is vanquished, pride and vain-
  glory remain;
When the mind is detached and casts Maya away,
  still it clings to the letter.
Kabir says, "Listen to me, dear Sadhu! the true
  path is rarely found."

VI

I. 83. candā jhalkai yahi ghaṭ māhīn

THE moon shines in my body, but my blind
    eyes cannot see it:
The moon is within me, and so is the sun.
The unstruck drum of Eternity is sounded within
    me; but my deaf ears cannot hear it.

So long as man clamours for the *I* and the *Mine*,
    his works are as naught:
When all love of the *I* and the *Mine* is dead, then
    the work of the Lord is done.
For work has no other aim than the getting of
    knowledge:
When that comes, then work is put away.

The flower blooms for the fruit: when the fruit
    comes, the flower withers.
The musk is in the deer, but it seeks it not within
    itself: it wanders in quest of grass.

VII

I. 85. sādho, Brahm alakh lakhāyā

WHEN He Himself reveals Himself,
    Brahma brings into manifestation That
which can never be seen.
As the seed is in the plant, as the shade is in the
    tree, as the void is in the sky, as infinite
    forms are in the void—

So from beyond the Infinite, the Infinite comes;
   and from the Infinite the finite extends.

The creature is in Brahma, and Brahma is in the
   creature: they are ever distinct, yet ever
   united.
He Himself is the tree, the seed, and the germ.
He Himself is the flower, the fruit, and the shade.
He Himself is the sun, the light, and the lighted.
He Himself is Brahma, creature, and Maya.
He Himself is the manifold form, the infinite
   space;
He is the breath, the word, and the meaning.
He Himself is the limit and the limitless: and
   beyond both the limited and the limitless
   is He, the Pure Being.
He is the Immanent Mind in Brahma and in the
   creature.

The Supreme Soul is seen within the soul,
The Point is seen within the Supreme Soul,
And within the Point, the reflection is seen again.
Kabir is blest because he has this supreme vision!

VIII

I. 101. *is ghaṭ antar bāg bagīce*

WITHIN this earthern vessel are bowers
   and groves, and within it is the Creator:
Within this vessel are the seven oceans and the
   unnumbered stars.

The touchstone and the jewel-appraiser are within;
And within this vessel the Eternal soundeth, and
the spring wells up.
Kabir says: "Listen to me, my friend! My be-
loved Lord is within."

IX

I. 104. *aisā lo nahīn taisā lo*

O HOW may I ever express that secret word?
O how can I say He is not like this, and
He is like that?
If I say that He is within me, the universe is
ashamed:
If I say that He is without me, it is falsehood.
He makes the inner and the outer worlds to be
indivisibly one;
The conscious and the unconscious, both are His
footstools.
He is neither manifest nor hidden, He is neither
revealed nor unrevealed:
There are no words to tell that which He is.

X

I. 121. *tohi mori lagan lagāye re phakīr wā*

TO Thee Thou hast drawn my love, O Fakir!
I was sleeping in my own chamber, and
Thou didst awaken me; striking me with
Thy voice, O Fakir!

I was drowning in the deeps of the ocean of this
world, and Thou didst save me: upholding
me with Thine arm, O Fakir!
Only one word and no second—and Thou hast
made me tear off all my bonds, O Fakir!
Kabir says, " Thou hast united Thy heart to my
heart, O Fakir!"

XI

I. 131. *niś din khelat rahī sakhiyān sang*

I PLAYED day and night with my comrades,
and now I am greatly afraid.
So high is my Lord's palace, my heart trembles
to mount its stairs: yet I must not be shy,
if I would enjoy His love.
My heart must cleave to my Lover; I must with-
draw my veil, and meet Him with all my
body:
Mine eyes must perform the ceremony of the
lamps of love.
Kabir says: " Listen to me, friend: he under-
stands who loves. If you feel not love's
longing for your Beloved One, it is vain to
adorn your body, vain to put unguent on
your eyelids."

XII

II. 24. *haṃsā, kaho purātan bāt*

TELL me, O Swan, your ancient tale.
From what land do you come, O Swan? to
what shore will you fly?
Where would you take your rest, O Swan, and
what do you seek?

Even this morning, O Swan, awake, arise, follow
me!
There is a land where no doubt nor sorrow have
rule: where the terror of Death is no more.
There the woods of spring are a-bloom, and the
fragrant scent "He is I" is borne on the
wind:
There the bee of the heart is deeply immersed,
and desires no other joy.

XIII

II. 37. *angaḍhiyā devā*

O LORD Increate, who will serve Thee?
Every votary offers his worship to the God
of his own creation: each day he receives
service—
None seek Him, the Perfect: Brahma, the Indi-
visible Lord.
They believe in ten Avatars; but no Avatar can
be the Infinite Spirit, for he suffers the re-
sults of his deeds:

The Supreme One must be other than this.
The Yogi, the Sanyasi, the Ascetics, are disputing
    one with another:
Kabir says, "O brother! he who has seen that
    radiance of love, he is saved."

XIV

II. 56. *dariyā kī lahar dariyāo hai jī*

THE river and its waves are one surf: where
is the difference between the river and its
waves?
When the wave rises, it is the water; and when
    it falls, it is the same water again. Tell me,
    Sir, where is the distinction?
Because it has been named as wave, shall it no
    longer be considered as water?

Within the Supreme Brahma, the worlds are being
    told like beads:
Look upon that rosary with the eyes of wisdom.

XV

II. 57. *jānh khelat vasant riturāj*

WHERE Spring, the lord of the seasons,
reigneth, there the Unstruck Music sounds
of itself,
There the streams of light flow in all directions;
Few are the men who can cross to that shore!

There, where millions of Krishnas stand with
    hands folded,
Where millions of Vishnus bow their heads,
Where millions of Brahmās are reading the Vedas,
Where millions of Shivas are lost in contemplation,
Where millions of Indras dwell in the sky,
Where the demi-gods and the munis are un-
    numbered,
Where millions of Saraswatis, Goddess of Music,
    play on the vina—
There is my Lord self-revealed: and the scent of
    sandàl and flowers dwells in those deeps.

XVI

II. 59. *jānh cet acet khambh dōū*

BETWEEN the poles of the conscious and
    the unconscious, there has the mind made
    a swing:
Thereon hang all beings and all worlds, and that
    swing never ceases its sway.
Millions of beings are there: the sun and the
    moon in their courses are there:
Millions of ages pass, and the swing goes on.
All swing! the sky and the earth and the air and
    the water; and the Lord Himself taking
    form:
And the sight of this has made Kabir a servant.

XVII

II. 61. grah candra tapan jot barat hai

THE light of the sun, the moon, and the stars
shines bright:
The melody of love swells forth, and the rhythm
of love's detachment beats the time.
Day and night, the chorus of music fills the heav-
ens; and Kabir says
"My Beloved One gleams like the lightning flash
in the sky."

Do you know how the moments perform their
adoration?
Waving its row of lamps, the universe sings in
worship day and night,
There are the hidden banner and the secret
canopy:
There the sound of the unseen bells is heard.
Kabir says: "There adoration never ceases; there
the Lord of the Universe sitteth on His
throne."

The whole world does its works and commits its
errors: but few are the lovers who know
the Beloved.
The devout seeker is he who mingles in his heart
the double currents of love and detach-
ment, like the mingling of the streams of
Ganges and Jumna;

In his heart the sacred water flows day and night;
    and thus the round of births and deaths is
    brought to an end.

Behold what wonderful rest is in the Supreme
    Spirit! and he enjoys it, who makes him-
    self meet for it.
Held by the cords of love, the swing of the Ocean
    of Joy sways to and fro; and a mighty
    sound breaks forth in song.
See what a lotus blooms there without water! and
    Kabir says
" My heart's bee drinks its nectar."

What a wonderful lotus it is, that blooms at the
    heart of the spinning wheel of the universe!
    Only a few pure souls know of its true
    delight.
Music is all around it, and there the heart par-
    takes of the joy of the Infinite Sea.
Kabir says: "Dive thou into that Ocean of sweet-
    ness: thus let all errors of life and of death
    flee away."

Behold how the thirst of the five senses is quenched
    there! and the three forms of misery are
    no more!
Kabir says: " It is the sport of the Unattainable
    One: look within, and behold how the
    moon-beams of that Hidden One shine in
    you."

There falls the rhythmic beat of life and death:
Rapture wells forth, and all space is radiant with
     light.
There the Unstruck Music is sounded; it is the
     music of the love of the three worlds.
There millions of lamps of sun and of moon are
     burning;
There the drum beats, and the lover swings in
     play.
There love-songs resound, and light rains in
     showers; and the worshipper is entranced
     in the taste of the heavenly nectar.
Look upon life and death; there is no separation
     between them,
The right hand and the left hand are one and the
     same.
Kabir says: "There the wise man is speechless;
     for this truth may never be found in Vedas
     or in books."

I have had my Seat on the Self-poised One,
I have drunk of the Cup of the Ineffable,
I have found the Key of the Mystery,
I have reached the Root of Union.
Travelling by no track, I have come to the Sorrow-
     less Land: very easily has the mercy of the
     great Lord come upon me.
They have sung of Him as infinite and unattain-
     able: but I in my meditations have seen
     Him without sight.

That is indeed the sorrowless land, and none
   know the path that leads there:
Only he who is on that path has surely transcended
   all sorrow.
Wonderful is that land of rest, to which no merit
   can win;
It is the wise who has seen it, it is the wise who
   has sung of it.
This is the Ultimate Word: but can any ex-
   press its marvellous savour? He who has
   savoured it once, he knows what joy it can
   give.
Kabir says: " Knowing it, the ignorant man be-
   comes wise, and the wise man becomes
   speechless and silent,
The worshipper is utterly inebriated,
His wisdom and his detachment are made per-
   fect;
He drinks from the cup of the inbreathings and
   the outbreathings of love."

There the whole sky is filled with sound, and
   there that music is made without fingers
   and without strings;
There the game of pleasure and pain does not
   cease.
Kabir says: "If you merge your life in the Ocean
   of Life, you will find your life in the
   Supreme Land of Bliss."

What a frenzy of ecstacy there is in every hour!
  and the worshipper is pressing out and
  drinking the essence of the hours: he lives
  in the life of Brahma.
I speak truth, for I have accepted truth in life; I
  am now attached to truth, I have swept all
  tinsel away.
Kabir says: "Thus is the worshipper set free
  from fear; thus have all errors of life and
  of death left him."

There the sky is filled with music:
There it rains nectar:
There the harp-strings jingle, and there the drums
  beat.
What a secret splendour is there, in the mansion
  of the sky!
There no mention is made of the rising and the
  setting of the sun;
In the ocean of manifestation, which is the light
  of love, day and night are felt to be one.
Joy for ever, no sorrow, no struggle!
There have I seen joy filled to the brim, perfection
  of joy;
No place for error is there.
Kabir says: "There have I witnessed the sport of
  One Bliss!"

I have known in my body the sport of the
  universe: I have escaped from the error
  of this world.

The inward and the outward are become as one
 sky, the Infinite and the finite are uni-
 ted: I am drunken with the sight of this
 All!
This Light of Thine fulfils the universe: the
 lamp of love that burns on the salver of
 knowledge.
Kabir says: "There error cannot enter, and
 the conflict of life and death is felt no
 more."

XVIII

II. 77. *maddh ākās āp jahān baiṭhe*

THE middle region of the sky, wherein the
 spirit dwelleth, is radiant with the music
 of light;
There, where the pure and white music blossoms,
 my Lord takes His delight.
In the wondrous effulgence of each hair of His
 body, the brightness of millions of suns and
 of moons is lost.
On that shore there is a city, where the rain of
 nectar pours and pours, and never ceases.
Kabir says: "Come, O Dharmadas! and see my
 great Lord's Durbar."

XIX

II. 20. paramātam guru nikaṭ virājaiṇ

O MY heart! the Supreme Spirit, the great
Master, is near you: wake, oh wake!
Run to the feet of your Beloved: for your Lord
stands near to your head.
You have slept for unnumbered ages; this morn-
ing will you not wake?

XX

II. 22. man tu pār utar kānh jaiho

TO what shore would you cross, O my heart?
there is no traveller before you, there is no
road:
Where is the movement, where is the rest, on that
shore?
There is no water; no boat, no boatman, is
there;
There is not so much as a rope to tow the boat,
nor a man to draw it.
No earth, no sky, no time, no thing, is there: no
shore, no ford!
There, there is neither body nor mind: and where
is the place that shall still the thirst of the
soul? You shall find naught in that empti-
ness.

Be strong, and enter into your own body: for
there your foothold is firm. Consider it
well, O my heart! go not elsewhere.
Kabir says: "Put all imaginations away, and
stand fast in that which you are."

XXI

II. 33. *ghar ghar dīpak barai*

LAMPS burn in every house, O blind one!
and you cannot see them.
One day your eyes shall suddenly be opened, and
you shall see: and the fetters of death will
fall from you.
There is nothing to say or to hear, there is no-
thing to do: it is he who is living, yet dead,
who shall never die again.

Because he lives in solitude, therefore the Yogi
says that his home is far away.
Your Lord is near: yet you are climbing the
palm-tree to seek Him.
The Brahman priest goes from house to house and
initiates people into faith:
Alas! the true fountain of life is beside you, and
you have set up a stone to worship.
Kabir says: "I may never express how sweet my
Lord is. Yoga and the telling of beads,
virtue and vice—these are naught to Him."

XXII

II. 38.   *sādho, so satgur mohi bhāwai*

O BROTHER, my heart yearns for that true
   Guru, who fills the cup of true love, and
   drinks of it himself, and offers it then to me.
He removes the veil from the eyes, and gives the
   true Vision of Brahma:
He reveals the worlds in Him, and makes me to
   hear the Unstruck Music:
He shows joy and sorrow to be one:
He fills all utterance with love.
Kabir says: "Verily he has no fear, who has such
   a Guru to lead him to the shelter of safety!"

XXIII

II. 40.   *tinwir sāñjh kā gahirā āwai*

THE shadows of evening fall thick and deep,
   and the darkness of love envelops the
   body and the mind.
Open the window to the west, and be lost in the
   sky of love;
Drink the sweet honey that steeps the petals of
   the lotus of the heart.
Receive the waves in your body: what splendour
   is in the region of the sea!
Hark! the sounds of conches and bells are rising.
Kabir says: "O brother, behold! the Lord is in
   this vessel of my body."

XXIV

II. 48. *jis se rahani apār jagat men*

MORE than all else do I cherish at heart
that love which makes me to live a limitless
life in this world.

It is like the lotus, which lives in the water and
blooms in the water: yet the water cannot
touch its petals, they open beyond its reach.

It is like a wife, who enters the fire at the bidding
of love. She burns and lets others grieve,
yet never dishonours love.

This ocean of the world is hard to cross: its
waters are very deep. Kabir says: "Listen
to me, O Sadhu! few there are who have
reached its end."

XXV

II. 45. *Hari ne apnā āp chipāyā*

MY Lord hides Himself, and my Lord won-
derfully reveals Himself:

My Lord has encompassed me with hardness, and
my Lord has cast down my limitations.

My Lord brings to me words of sorrow and words
of joy, and He Himself heals their strife.

I will offer my body and mind to my Lord: I
will give up my life, but never can I forget
my Lord!

XXVI

II. 75. *ōṇkār siwāe kōī sirjai*

ALL things are created by the Om;
The love-form is His body.
He is without form, without quality, without decay:
Seek thou union with Him!

But that formless God takes a thousand forms in
the eyes of His creatures:
He is pure and indestructible,
His form is infinite and fathomless,
He dances in rapture, and waves of form arise
from His dance.
The body and the mind cannot contain themselves,
when they are touched by His great joy.
He is immersed in all consciousness, all joys, and
all sorrows;
He has no beginning and no end;
He holds all within His bliss.

XXVII

II. 81. *satgur sōī dayā kar dīnhā*

IT is the mercy of my true Guru that has made
me to know the unknown;
I have learned from Him how to walk without
feet, to see without eyes, to hear without
ears, to drink without mouth, to fly without
wings;

I have brought my love and my meditation into
the land where there is no sun and moon,
nor day and night.
Without eating, I have tasted of the sweetness of
nectar; and without water, I have quenched
my thirst.
Where there is the response of delight, there is
the fullness of joy. Before whom can that
joy be uttered?
Kabir says: " The Guru is great beyond words,
and great is the good fortune of the dis-
ciple."

XXVIII

II. 85. *nirguṇ āge sarguṇ nācai*

BEFORE the Unconditioned, the Conditioned
dances:
" Thou and I are one! " this trumpet proclaims.
The Guru comes, and bows down before the dis-
ciple:
This is the greatest of wonders.

XXIX

II. 87. *Kabīr kab se bhaye vairāgī*

GORAKHNATH asks Kabir:
" Tell me, O Kabir, when did your vocation
begin? Where did your love have its rise?"

Kabir answers:

" When He whose forms are manifold had not be-
gun His play: when there was no Guru, and
no disciple: when the world was not spread
out: when the Supreme One was alone—
Then I became an ascetic; then, O Gorakh, my
love was drawn to Brahma.
Brahmā did not hold the crown on his head; the
god Vishnu was not anointed as king; the
power of Shiva was still unborn; when I
was instructed in Yoga.

"I became suddenly revealed in Benares, and
Ramananda illumined me;
I brought with me the thirst for the Infinite, and
I have come for the meeting with Him.
In simplicity will I unite with the Simple One;
my love will surge up.
O Gorakh, march thou with His music!"

XXX

II. 95. *yā tarvar meṇ ek pakherū*

O N this tree is a bird: it dances in the joy of life.
None knows where it is: and who knows
what the burden of its music may be?
Where the branches throw a deep shade, there
does it have its nest: and it comes in the
evening and flies away in the morning, and
says not a word of that which it means.

None tell me of this bird that sings within me.
It is neither coloured nor colourless: it has neither
 form nor outline:
It sits in the shadow of love.
It dwells within the Unattainable, the Infinite,
 and the Eternal; and no one marks when
 it comes and goes.
Kabir says: "O brother Sadhu! deep is the mys-
 tery. Let wise men seek to know where
 rests that bird."

XXXI

II. 100. *niś din sālai ghāw*

A SORE pain troubles me day and night, and
 I cannot sleep;
I long for the meeting with my Beloved, and my
 father's house gives me pleasure no more.

The gates of the sky are opened, the temple is
 revealed:
I meet my husband, and leave at His feet the
 offering of my body and my mind.

XXXII

II. 103. *nāco re mero man, matta hoy*

DANCE, my heart! dance to-day with joy.
 The strains of love fill the days and the
 nights with music, and the world is listen-
 ing to its melodies:

Mad with joy, life and death dance to the rhythm
of this music. The hills and the sea and
the earth dance. The world of man dances
in laughter and tears.
Why put on the robe of the monk, and live aloof
from the world in lonely pride?
Behold! my heart dances in the delight of a
hundred arts; and the Creator is well
pleased.

XXXIII

II. 105. *man mast huā tab kyon bole*

WHERE is the need of words, when love
has made drunken the heart?
I have wrapped the diamond in my cloak; why
open it again and again?
When its load was light, the pan of the balance
went up: now it is full, where is the need
for weighing?
The swan has taken its flight to the lake beyond
the mountains; why should it search for
the pools and ditches any more?
Your Lord dwells within you: why need your
outward eyes be opened?
Kabir says: "Listen, my brother! my Lord, who
ravishes my eyes, has united Himself with
me."

XXXIV

II. 110. *mohi tohi lāgī kaise chuṭe*

HOW could the love between Thee and me sever?

As the leaf of the lotus abides on the water: so thou art my Lord, and I am Thy servant.

As the night-bird Chakor gazes all night at the moon: so Thou art my Lord and I am Thy servant.

From the beginning until the ending of time, there is love between Thee and me; and how shall such love be extinguished?

Kabir says: "As the river enters into the ocean, so my heart touches Thee."

XXXV

II. 113. *vālam, āwo hamāre geh re*

MY body and my mind are grieved for the want of Thee;

O my Beloved! come to my house.

When people say I am Thy bride, I am ashamed; for I have not touched Thy heart with my heart.

Then what is this love of mine? I have no taste for food, I have no sleep; my heart is ever restless within doors and without.

As water is to the thirsty, so is the lover to the
bride. Who is there that will carry my
news to my Beloved?
Kabir is restless: he is dying for sight of Him.

XXXVI

II. 126. *jāg piyārī, ab kān sowai*

O FRIEND, awake, and sleep no more!
The night is over and gone, would you lose
your day also?
Others, who have wakened, have received jewels;
O foolish woman! you have lost all whilst you
slept.
Your lover is wise, and you are foolish, O woman!
You never prepared the bed of your husband:
O mad one! you passed your time in silly play.
Your youth was passed in vain, for you did not
know your Lord;
Wake, wake! See! your bed is empty: He left
you in the night.
Kabir says: "Only she wakes, whose heart is
pierced with the arrow of His music."

XXXVII

I. 36. *sūr parkās, tānh rain kahān pāïye*

WHERE is the night, when the sun is
shining? If it is night, then the sun with-
draws its light.

Where knowledge is, can ignorance endure? If
  there be ignorance, then knowledge must
  die.
If there be lust, how can love be there? Where
  there is love, there is no lust.

Lay hold on your sword, and join in the fight.
  Fight, O my brother, as long as life lasts.
Strike off your enemy's head, and there make an
  end of him quickly: then come, and bow
  your head at your King's Durbar.
He who is brave, never forsakes the battle: he
  who flies from it is no true fighter.
In the field of this body a great war goes forward,
  against passion, anger, pride, and greed:
It is in the kingdom of truth, contentment and
  purity, that this battle is raging; and the
  sword that rings forth most loudly is the
  sword of His Name.
Kabir says: "When a brave knight takes the field,
  a host of cowards is put to flight.
It is a hard fight and a weary one, this fight of the
  truth-seeker: for the vow of the truth-
  seeker is more hard than that of the warrior,
  or of the widowed wife who would follow
  her husband.
For the warrior fights for a few hours, and the
  widow's struggle with death is soon ended:
But the truth-seeker's battle goes on day and
  night, as long as life lasts it never ceases."

XXXVIII

I. 50. *bhram kā tālā lagā mahal re*

THE lock of error shuts the gate, open it with
the key of love:
Thus, by opening the door, thou shalt wake the
Beloved.
Kabir says: " O brother! do not pass by such good
fortune as this."

XXXIX

I. 59. *sādho, yah tan ṭhāṭh tanvure kā*

O FRIEND! this body is His lyre;
He tightens its strings, and draws from it
the melody of Brahma.
If the strings snap and the keys slacken, then to
dust must this instrument of dust return:
Kabir says: "None but Brahma can evoke its
melodies."

XL

I. 65. *avadhū bhūle ko ghar lāwe*

HE is dear to me indeed who can call back
the wanderer to his home. In the home is
the true union, in the home is enjoyment of
life: why should I forsake my home and
wander in the forest? If Brahma helps me
to realize truth, verily I will find both
bondage and deliverance in home.

He is dear to me indeed who has power to dive
deep into Brahma; whose mind loses itself
with ease in His contemplation.

He is dear to me who knows Brahma, and can
dwell on His supreme truth in meditation;
and who can play the melody of the Infinite
by uniting love and renunciation in life.

Kabir says: "The home is the abiding place; in
the home is reality; the home helps to
attain Him Who is real. So stay where you
are, and all things shall come to you in
time."

XLI

I. 76. *santo, sahaj samādh bhalī*

O SADHU! the simple union is the best.
Since the day when I met with my Lord,
there has been no end to the sport of our
love.

I shut not my eyes, I close not my ears, I do not
mortify my body;

I see with eyes open and smile, and behold His
beauty everywhere:

I utter His Name, and whatever I see, it reminds
me of Him; whatever I do, it becomes His
worship.

The rising and the setting are one to me; all
contradictions are solved.

Wherever I go, I move round Him,

All I achieve is His service:
When I lie down, I lie prostrate at His feet.

He is the only adorable one to me: I have none
    other.
My tongue has left off impure words, it sings His
    glory day and night:
Whether I rise or sit down, I can never forget
    Him; for the rhythm of His music beats
    in my ears.
Kabir says: "My heart is frenzied, and I disclose
    in my soul what is hidden. I am immersed
    in that one great bliss which transcends all
    pleasure and pain."

XLII

I. 79.   tīrath men̤ to sab pānī hai

THERE is nothing but water at the holy
    bathing places; and I know that they are
    useless, for I have bathed in them.
The images are all lifeless, they cannot speak; I
    know, for I have cried aloud to them.
The Purana and the Koran are mere words;
    lifting up the curtain, I have seen.
Kabir gives utterance to the words of experience;
    and he knows very well that all other things
    are untrue.

XLIII

I. 82. pānī vic mīn piyāsī

I LAUGH when I hear that the fish in the
water is thirsty:
You do not see that the Real is in your home, and
you wander from forest to forest listlessly!
Here is the truth! Go where you will, to Benares
or to Mathura; if you do not find your
soul, the world is unreal to you.

XLIV

I. 93. gagan maṭh gaib nisān gaḍe

THE Hidden Banner is planted in the temple
of the sky; there the blue canopy decked
with the moon and set with bright jewels
is spread.
There the light of the sun and the moon is shining:
still your mind to silence before that splen-
dour.
Kabir says: " He who has drunk of this nectar,
wanders like one who is mad."

XLV

I. 97. sādho, ko hai kānh se āyo

WHO are you, and whence do you come?
Where dwells that Supreme Spirit, and
how does He have His sport with all
created things?

The fire is in the wood; but who awakens it suddenly? Then it turns to ashes, and where goes the force of the fire?

The true guru teaches that He has neither limit nor infinitude.

Kabir says: " Brahma suits His language to the understanding of His hearer."

XLVI

I. 98. *sādho, sahajai kāyā śodho*

O SADHU! purify your body in the simple way.

As the seed is within the banyan tree, and within the seed are the flowers, the fruits, and the shade:

So the germ is within the body, and within that germ is the body again.

The fire, the air, the water, the earth, and the aether; you cannot have these outside of Him.

O Kazi, O Pundit, consider it well: what is there that is not in the soul?

The water-filled pitcher is placed upon water, it has water within and without.

It should not be given a name, lest it call forth the error of dualism.

Kabir says: "Listen to the Word, the Truth, which is your essence. He speaks the Word to Himself; and He Himself is the Creator."

XLVII

I. 102. *tarvar ek mūl bin ṭhāḍā*

THERE is a strange tree, which stands with-
out roots and bears fruits without blos-
soming;

It has no branches and no leaves, it is lotus all
over.

Two birds sing there; one is the Guru, and the
other the disciple:

The disciple chooses the manifold fruits of life
and tastes them, and the Guru beholds
him in joy.

What Kabir says is hard to understand: The bird
is beyond seeking, yet it is most clearly
visible. The Formless is in the midst of all
forms. I sing the glory of forms."

XLVIII

I. 107. *calat mansā acal kīnhī*

I HAVE stilled my restless mind, and my heart
is radiant: for in That-ness I have seen
beyond That-ness, in company I have seen
the Comrade Himself.

Living in bondage, I have set myself free: I have
broken away from the clutch of all narrow-
ness.

Kabir says: "I have attained the unattainable, and
my heart is coloured with the colour of love."

XLIX

I. 105. *jo dīsai, so to hai nāhiṇ*

THAT which you see is not: and for that
which is, you have no words.
Unless you see, you believe not: what is told you
you cannot accept.
He who is discerning knows by the word; and
the ignorant stands gaping.
Some contemplate the Formless, and others medi-
tate on form: but the wise man knows that
Brahma is beyond both.
That beauty of His is not seen of the eye: that
metre of His is not heard of the ear.
Kabir says: " He who has found both love and
renunciation never descends to death."

L

I. 126. *muralī bajat akhaṇḍ sadāye*

THE flute of the Infinite is played without
ceasing, and its sound is love:
When love renounces all limits, it reaches truth.
How widely the fragrance spreads! It has no end,
nothing stands in its way.
The form of this melody is bright like a million
suns: incomparably sounds the vina, the
vina of the notes of truth.

LI

I. 129. *sakhiyo, ham hūṇ bhāī vālamāsī*

DEAR friend, I am eager to meet my Be-
loved! My youth has flowered, and the
pain of separation from Him troubles my
breast.

I am wandering yet in the alleys of knowledge
without purpose, but I have received His
news in these alleys of knowledge.

I have a letter from my Beloved: in this letter
is an unutterable message, and now my
fear of death is done away.

Kabir says: "O my loving friend! I have got for
my gift the Deathless One."

LII

I. 130. *sāīṇ bin dard kareje hoy*

WHEN I am parted from my Beloved, my
heart is full of misery: I have no comfort
in the day, I have no sleep in the night.
To whom shall I tell my sorrow?

The night is dark; the hours slip by. Because my
Lord is absent, I start up and tremble with
fear.

Kabir says: "Listen, my friend! there is no other
satisfaction, save in the encounter with the
Beloved."

LIII

I. 122. *kaun murali sabd sun anand bhayo*

WHAT is that flute whose music thrills me
with joy?
The flame burns without a lamp;
The lotus blossoms without a root;
Flowers bloom in clusters;
The moon-bird is devoted to the moon;
With all its heart the rain-bird longs for the
shower of rain;
But upon whose love does the Lover concentrate
His entire life?

LIV

I. 112. *sunta nahi dhun ki khabar*

HAVE you not heard the tune which the
Unstruck Music is playing? In the midst
of the chamber the harp of joy is gently
and sweetly played; and where is the need
of going without to hear it?
If you have not drunk of the nectar of that One
Love, what boots it though you should
purge yourself of all stains?
The Kazi is searching the words of the Koran,
and instructing others: but if his heart be
not steeped in that love, what does it avail,
though he be a teacher of men?

The Yogi dyes his garments with red: but if he
    knows naught of that colour of love, what
    does it avail though his garments be tinted?
Kabir says: "Whether I be in the temple or the
    balcony, in the camp or in the flower
    garden, I tell you truly that every moment
    my Lord is taking His delight in me."

LV

I. 73. *bhakti kā mārag jhīnā re*

SUBTLE is the path of love!
    Therein there is no asking and no not-asking,
There one loses one's self at His feet,
There one is immersed in the joy of the seeking:
    plunged in the deeps of love as the fish in
    the water.
The lover is never slow in offering his head for
    his Lord's service.
Kabir declares the secret of this love.

LVI

I. 68. *bhāī koī satguru sant kahāwai*

HE is the real Sadhu, who can reveal the
    form of the Formless to the vision of these
    eyes:
Who teaches the simple way of attaining Him,
    that is other than rites or ceremonies:
Who does not make you close the doors, and hold
    the breath, and renounce the world:

Who makes you perceive the Supreme Spirit
    wherever the mind attaches itself:
Who teaches you to be still in the midst of all
    your activities.
Ever immersed in bliss, having no fear in his
    mind, he keeps the spirit of union in the
    midst of all enjoyments.

The infinite dwelling of the Infinite Being is
    everywhere: in earth, water, sky, and air:
Firm as the thunderbolt, the seat of the seeker is
    established above the void.
He who is within is without: I see Him and none
    else.

LVII

I. 66. sādho, śabd sādhanā kījaı

RECEIVE that Word from which the Uni-
    verse springeth!
That Word is the Guru; I have heard it, and
    become the disciple.
How many are there who know the meaning of
    that Word?

O Sadhu! practise that Word!
The Vedas and the Puranas proclaim it,
The world is established in it,
The Rishis and devotees speak of it:
But none knows the mystery of the Word.

The householder leaves his house when he hears it,
The ascetic comes back to love when he hears it,
The Six Philosophies expound it,
The Spirit of Renunciation points to that Word,
From that Word the world-form has sprung,
That Word reveals all.
Kabir says: "But who knows whence the Word
    cometh?"

LVIII

I. 63. *pī le pyālā, ho matwālā*

EMPTY the Cup! O be drunken!
    Drink the divine nectar of His Name!
Kabir says: "Listen to me, dear Sadhu!
From the sole of the foot to the crown of the head
    this mind is filled with poison."

LIX

I. 52. *khasm na cīnhai bāwarī*

O MAN, if thou dost not know thine own
    Lord, whereof art thou so proud?
Put thy cleverness away: mere words shall never
    unite thee to Him.
Do not deceive thyself with the witness of the
    Scriptures:
Love is something other than this, and he who
    has sought it truly has found it.

LX

I. 56. *sukh sindh kī sair kā*

THE savour of wandering in the ocean of
     deathless life has rid me of all my asking:
As the tree is in the seed, so all diseases are in
     this asking.

LXI

I. 48. *sukh sāgar men āīke*

WHEN at last you are come to the ocean of
      happiness, do not go back thirsty.
Wake, foolish man! for Death stalks you. Here
     is pure water before you; drink it at every
     breath.
Do not follow the mirage on foot, but thirst for
     the nectar;
Dhruva, Prahlad, and Shukadeva have drunk of it,
     and also Raidas has tasted it:
The saints are drunk with love, their thirst is for
     love.
Kabir says: "Listen to me, brother! The nest of
     fear is broken.
Not for a moment have you come face to face with
     the world:
You are weaving your bondage of falsehood, your
     words are full of deception:

With the load of desires which you hold on your
head, how can you be light?"
Kabir says: "Keep within you truth, detachment,
and love."

LXII

I. 35. *sati ko kaun śikhāwtā hai*

WHO has ever taught the widowed wife to
burn herself on the pyre of her dead
husband?
And who has ever taught love to find bliss in
renunciation?

LXIII

I. 39. *are man, dhīraj kāhe na dharai*

WHY so impatient, my heart?
He who watches over birds, beasts, and
insects,
He who cared for you whilst you were yet in
your mother's womb,
Shall He not care for you now that you are come
forth?
Oh my heart, how could you turn from the smile
of your Lord and wander so far from Him?
You have left your Beloved and are thinking of
others: and this is why all your work is in
vain.

LXIV

I. 117. sāïn se lagan kaṭhin hai, bhāī

HOW hard it is to meet my Lord!
    The rain-bird wails in thirst for the rain:
    almost she dies of her longing, yet she
    would have none other water than the rain.
Drawn by the love of music, the deer moves
    forward: she dies as she listens to the
    music, yet she shrinks not in fear.
The widowed wife sits by the body of her dead
    husband: she is not afraid of the fire.
Put away all fear for this poor body.

LXV

I. 22. jab main bhūlā, re bhāī

O BROTHER! when I was forgetful, my true
    Guru showed me the Way.
Then I left off all rites and ceremonies, I bathed
    no more in the holy water:
Then I learned that it was I alone who was mad,
    and the whole world beside me was sane;
    and I had disturbed these wise people.
From that time forth I knew no more how to roll
    in the dust in obeisance:
I do not ring the temple bell:
I do not set the idol on its throne:
I do not worship the image with flowers.

It is not the austerities that mortify the flesh
   which are pleasing to the Lord,
When you leave off your clothes and kill your
   senses, you do not please the Lord:
The man who is kind and who practises righteous-
   ness, who remains passive amidst the affairs
   of the world, who considers all creatures
   on earth as his own self,
He attains the Immortal Being, the true God is
   ever with him.
Kabir says: "He attains the true Name whose
   words are pure, and who is free from pride
   and conceit."

LXVI

I. 20. *man na rangāye*

THE Yogi dyes his garments, instead of
   dyeing his mind in the colours of love:
He sits within the temple of the Lord, leaving
   Brahma to worship a stone.
He pierces holes in his ears, he has a great beard
   and matted locks, he looks like a goat:
He goes forth into the wilderness, killing all his
   desires, and turns himself into an eunuch:
He shaves his head and dyes his garments; he
   reads the Gita and becomes a mighty talker.
Kabir says: "You are going to the doors of death,
   bound hand and foot!"

LXVII

I. 9. *nā jāne sāhab kaisā hai*

I DO not know what manner of God is mine.
The Mullah cries aloud to Him: and why? Is
    your Lord deaf? The subtle anklets that
    ring on the feet of an insect when it moves
    are heard of Him.
Tell your beads, paint your forehead with the
    mark of your God, and wear matted locks
    long and showy: but a deadly weapon is in
    your heart, and how shall you have God?

LXVIII

III. 102. *ham se rahā na jāy*

I HEAR the melody of His flute, and I cannot
    contain myself:
The flower blooms, though it is not spring; and
    already the bee has received its invitation.
The sky roars and the lightning flashes, the waves
    arise in my heart,
The rain falls; and my heart longs for my Lord.
Where the rhythm of the world rises and falls,
    thither my heart has reached:
There the hidden banners are fluttering in the air.
Kabir says: "My heart is dying, though it lives."

LXIX

III. 2. *jo khodā masjid vasat hai*

IF God be within the mosque, then to whom
does this world belong?
If Ram be within the image which you find upon
your pilgrimage, then who is there to know
what happens without?
Hari is in the East: Allah is in the West. Look
within your heart, for there you will find
both Karim and Ram;
All the men and women of the world are His
living forms.
Kabir is the child of Allah and of Ram: He is my
Guru, He is my Pir.

LXX

III. 9. *śīl santosh sadā samadrishṭi*

HE who is meek and contented, he who has
an equal vision, whose mind is filled with
the fullness of acceptance and of rest;
He who has seen Him and touched Him, he is
freed from all fear and trouble.
To him the perpetual thought of God is like
sandal paste smeared on the body, to him
nothing else is delight:
His work and his rest are filled with music: he
sheds abroad the radiance of love.

Kabir says: "Touch His feet, who is one and indivisible, immutable and peaceful; who fills all vessels to the brim with joy, and whose form is love."

LXXI

III. 13. *sādh sangat pītam*

GO thou to the company of the good, where the Beloved One has His dwelling place:
Take all thy thoughts and love and instruction from thence.
Let that assembly be burnt to ashes where His Name is not spoken!
Tell me, how couldst thou hold a wedding-feast, if the bridegroom himself were not there?
Waver no more, think only of the Beloved;
Set not thy heart on the worship of other gods, there is no worth in the worship of other masters.
Kabir deliberates and says: "Thus thou shalt never find the Beloved!"

LXXII

III. 26. *tor hīrā hirāilwā kīcaḍ meṇ*

THE jewel is lost in the mud, and all are seeking for it;
Some look for it in the east, and some in the west; some in the water and some amongst stones.

But the servant Kabir has appraised it at its true
value, and has wrapped it with care in the
end of the mantle of his heart.

LXXIII

III. 26. *āyau din gaune kā ho*

THE palanquin came to take me away to my
husband's home, and it sent through my
heart a thrill of joy;
But the bearers have brought me into the lonely
forest, where I have no one of my own.
O bearers, I entreat you by your feet, wait but a
moment longer: let me go back to my
kinsmen and friends, and take my leave of
them.
The servant Kabir sings: "O Sadhu! finish your
buying and selling, have done with your
good and your bad: for there are no mar-
kets and no shops in the land to which
you go."

LXXIV

III. 30. *are dil, prem nagar kā ant na pāyā*

O MY heart! you have not known all the
secrets of this city of love: in ignorance
you came, and in ignorance you return.

O my friend, what have you done with this life?
   You have taken on your head the burden
   heavy with stones, and who is to lighten it
   for you?
Your Friend stands on the other shore, but you
   never think in your mind how you may
   meet with Him:
The boat is broken, and yet you sit ever upon the
   bank; and thus you are beaten to no pur-
   pose by the waves.
The servant Kabir asks you to consider; who is
   there that shall befriend you at the last?
You are alone, you have no companion: you will
   suffer the consequences of your own deeds.

LXXV

III. 55. *ved kahe sargun ke āgĕ*

THE Vedas say that the Unconditioned stands
   beyond the world of Conditions.
O woman, what does it avail thee to dispute
   whether He is beyond all or in all?
See thou everything as thine own dwelling place:
   the mist of pleasure and pain can never
   spread there.
There Brahma is revealed day and night: there
   light is His garment, light is His seat, light
   rests on thy head.
Kabir says: "The Master, who is true, He is all
   light."

LXXVI

III. 48. *tū surat nain nihār*

OPEN your eyes of love, and see Him who
pervades this world! consider it well, and
know that this is your own country.

When you meet the true Guru, He will awaken
your heart;

He will tell you the secret of love and detachment,
and then you will know indeed that He
transcends this universe.

This world is the City of Truth, its maze of paths
enchants the heart:

We can reach the goal without crossing the road,
such is the sport unending.

Where the ring of manifold joys ever dances about
Him, there is the sport of Eternal Bliss.

When we know this, then all our receiving and
renouncing is over;

Thenceforth the heat of having shall never scorch
us more.

He is the Ultimate Rest unbounded:

He has spread His form of love throughout all
the world.

From that Ray which is Truth, streams of new
forms are perpetually springing: and He
pervades those forms.

All the gardens and groves and bowers are abounding with blossom; and the air breaks forth into ripples of joy.

There the swan plays a wonderful game,

There the Unstruck Music eddies around the Infinite One;

There in the midst the Throne of the Unheld is shining, whereon the great Being sits—

Millions of suns are shamed by the radiance of a single hair of His body.

On the harp of the road what true melodies are being sounded! and its notes pierce the heart:

There the Eternal Fountain is playing its endless life-streams of birth and death.

They call Him Emptiness who is the Truth of truths, in Whom all truths are stored!

There within Him creation goes forward, which is beyond all philosophy; for philosophy cannot attain to Him:

There is an endless world, O my Brother! and there is the Nameless Being, of whom nought can be said.

Only he knows it who has reached that region: it is other than all that is heard and said.

No form, no body, no length, no breadth is seen there: how can I tell you that which it is?

He comes to the Path of the Infinite on whom the
grace of the Lord descends: he is freed
from births and deaths who attains to
Him.
Kabir says: " It cannot be told by the words of
the mouth, it cannot be written on paper:
It is like a dumb person who tastes a sweet thing
—how shall it be explained? "

LXXVII

III. 60.   *cal haṃsā wā des jahān*

O MY heart! let us go to that country where
dwells the Beloved, the ravisher of my
heart!
There Love is filling her pitcher from the well,
yet she has no rope wherewith to draw
water;
There the clouds do not cover the sky, yet the
rain falls down in gentle showers:
O bodiless one! do not sit on your doorstep ; go
forth and bathe yourself in that rain!
There it is ever moonlight and never dark; and
who speaks of one sun only? that land is
illuminate with the rays of a million suns.

LXXVIII

III. 63. kahaiṇ Kabīr, śuno ho sādho

KABIR says: "O Sadhu! hear my deathless
words. If you want your own good, ex-
amine and consider them well.

You have estranged yourself from the Creator, of
whom you have sprung: you have lost
your reason, you have bought death.

All doctrines and all teachings are sprung from
Him, from Him they grow: know this for
certain, and have no fear.

Hear from me the tidings of this great truth!

Whose name do you sing, and on whom do you
meditate? O, come forth from this en-
tanglement!

He dwells at the heart of all things, so why take
refuge in empty desolation?

If you place the Guru at a distance from you, then
it is but the distance that you honour:

If indeed the Master be far away, then who is it
else that is creating this world?

When you think that He is not here, then you
wander further and further away, and seek
Him in vain with tears.

Where He is far off, there He is unattainable:
where He is near, He is very bliss.

Kabir says: "Lest His servant should suffer pain
He pervades him through and through."

Know yourself then, O Kabir; for He is in you
    from head to foot.
Sing with gladness, and keep your seat unmoved
    within your heart.

LXXIX

III. 66. *nā main dharmī nahīn adharmī*

I AM neither pious nor ungodly,
    I live neither by law nor by sense,
I am neither a speaker nor hearer,
I am neither a servant nor master,
I am neither bond nor free,
I am neither detached nor attached.
I am far from none: I am near to none.
I shall go neither to hell nor to heaven.
I do all works; yet I am apart from all works.
Few comprehend my meaning: he who can com-
    prehend it, he sits unmoved.
Kabir seeks neither to establish nor to destroy.

LXXX

III. 69. *satta nām hai sab ten nyārā*

THE true Name is like none other name!
    The distinction of the Conditioned from the
    Unconditioned is but a word:
The Unconditioned is the seed, the Conditioned
    is the flower and the fruit.
Knowledge is the branch, and the Name is the
    root.

Look, and see where the root is: happiness shall
　　be yours when you come to the root.
The root will lead you to the branch, the leaf, the
　　flower, and the fruit:
It is the encounter with the Lord, it is the attain-
　　ment of bliss, it is the reconciliation of the
　　Conditioned and the Unconditioned.

LXXXI

III. 74. *pratham ek jo āpai āp*

IN the beginning was He alone, sufficient unto
　　Himself: the formless, colourless, and un-
conditioned Being.
Then was there neither beginning, middle, nor end;
Then were no eyes, no darkness, no light;
Then were no ground, air, nor sky; no fire, water,
　　nor earth; no rivers like the Ganges and
　　the Jumna, no seas, oceans, and waves.
Then was neither vice nor virtue; scriptures there
　　were not, as the Vedas and Puranas, nor
　　as the Koran.
Kabir ponders in his mind and says, "Then
　　was there no activity: the Supreme Being
　　remained merged in the unknown depths
　　of His own self."

The Guru neither eats nor drinks, neither lives
　　nor dies:
Neither has He form, line, colour, nor vesture.

He who has neither caste nor clan nor anything
    else—how may I describe His glory?
He has neither form nor formlessness,
He has no name,
He has neither colour nor colourlessness,
He has no dwelling-place.

LXXXII

III. 76. *kahain Kabīr vicār ke*

KABIR ponders and says: "He who has
neither caste nor country, who is formless
and without quality, fills all space."
The Creator brought into being the Game of Joy:
    and from the word Om the Creation sprang.
The earth is His joy; His joy is the sky;
His joy is the flashing of the sun and the moon;
His joy is the beginning, the middle, and the end;
His joy is eyes, darkness, and light.
Oceans and waves are His joy: His joy the Saras-
    vati, the Jumna, and the Ganges.
The Guru is One: and life and death, union and
    separation, are all His plays of joy!
His play the land and water, the whole universe!
His play the earth and the sky!
In play is the Creation spread out, in play it is
    established. The whole world, says Kabir,
    rests in His play, yet still the Player re-
    mains unknown.

LXXXIII

III. 84.   *jhī jhī jantar bājai*

THE harp gives forth murmurous music; and
the dance goes on without hands and feet.
It is played without fingers, it is heard without
ears: for He is the ear, and He is the
listener.
The gate is locked, but within there is fragrance:
and there the meeting is seen of none.
The wise shall understand it.

LXXXIV

III. 89.   *mor phakīrwā māngi jāy*

THE Beggar goes a-begging, but I could not
even catch sight of Him:
And what shall I beg of the Beggar? He gives
without my asking.
Kabir says: "I am His own: now let that befall
which may befall!"

LXXXV

III. 90.   *naihar se jiyarā phāṭ re*

MY heart cries aloud for the house of my
lover; the open road and the shelter of a
roof are all one to her who has lost the
city of her husband.
My heart finds no joy in anything: my mind and
my body are distraught.

His palace has a million gates, but there is a vast
    ocean between it and me:
How shall I cross it, O friend? for endless is the
    outstretching of the path.

How wondrously this lyre is wrought! When its
    strings are rightly strung, it maddens the
    heart: but when the keys are broken and
    the strings are loosened, none regard it
    more.
I tell my parents with laughter that I must go to
    my Lord in the morning;
They are angry, for they do not want me to go,
    and they say: "She thinks she has gained
    such dominion over her husband that she
    can have whatsoever she wishes; and there-
    fore she is impatient to go to him."
Dear friend, lift my veil lightly now; for this is
    the night of love.
Kabir says: "Listen to me! My heart is eager to
    meet my lover: I lie sleepless upon my bed.
    Remember me early in the morning!"

LXXXVI

III. 96. *jīv mahal meṇ Śiv pahunwā*

SERVE your God, who has come into this
    temple of life!
Do not act the part of a madman, for the night is
    thickening fast.

He has awaited me for countless ages, for love
    of me He has lost His heart:
Yet I did not know the bliss that was so near to
    me, for my love was not yet awake.
But now, my Lover has made known to me the
    meaning of the note that struck my ear:
Now, my good fortune is come.
Kabir says : "Behold! how great is my good
    fortune! I have received the unending
    caress of my Beloved!"

LXXXVII

I. 71. *gagan ghaṭā ghaharānī, sādho*

CLOUDS thicken in the sky! O, listen to the
    deep voice of their roaring;
The rain comes from the east with its monotonous
    murmur.
Take care of the fences and boundaries of your
    fields, lest the rains overflow them;
Prepare the soil of deliverance, and let the creepers
    of love and renunciation be soaked in this
    shower.
It is the prudent farmer who will bring his harvest
    home; he shall fill both his vessels, and
    feed both the wise men and the saints.

LXXXVIII

III. 118. āj din ke main jāun balihārī

THIS day is dear to me above all other days,
for to-day the Beloved Lord is a guest in
my house;
My chamber and my courtyard are beautiful with
His presence.
My longings sing His Name, and they are become
lost in His great beauty:
I wash His feet, and I look upon His Face; and
I lay before Him as an offering my body,
my mind, and all that I have.
What a day of gladness is that day in which my
Beloved, who is my treasure, comes to my
house!
All evils fly from my heart when I see my Lord.
" My love has touched Him; my heart is longing
for the Name which is Truth."
Thus sings Kabîr, the servant of all servants.

LXXXIX

I. 100. koī suntā hai jñānī rāg gagan men

IS there any wise man who will listen to that
solemn music which arises in the sky?
For He, the Source of all music, makes all vessels
full fraught, and rests in fullness Himself.

He who is in the body is ever athirst, for he
    pursues that which is in part:
But ever there wells forth deeper and deeper the
    sound "He is this—this is He"; fusing
    love and renunciation into one.
Kabir says: "O brother! that is the Primal
    Word."

XC

I. 108. *main kā se būjhaun*

TO whom shall I go to learn about my Be-
    loved?
Kabir says: "As you never may find the forest if
    you ignore the tree, so He may never be
    found in abstractions."

XCI

III. 12. *samskirit bhāshā paḍhi līnhā*

I HAVE learned the Sanskrit language, so let
    all men call me wise:
But where is the use of this, when I am floating
    adrift, and parched with thirst, and burning
    with the heat of desire?
To no purpose do you bear on your head this load
    of pride and vanity.
Kabir says: "Lay it down in the dust, and go
    forth to meet the Beloved. Address Him
    as your Lord."

XCII

III. 110. *carkhā calai surat virahin kā*

THE woman who is parted from her lover
spins at the spinning wheel.

The city of the body arises in its beauty; and
within it the palace of the mind has been
built.

The wheel of love revolves in the sky, and the
seat is made of the jewels of knowledge:

What subtle threads the woman weaves, and
makes them fine with love and reverence!

Kabir says: "I am weaving the garland of day and
night. When my Lover comes and touches
me with His feet, I shall offer Him my
tears."

XCIII

III. 111. *koṭīn bhānu candra tārāgaṇ*

BENEATH the great umbrella of my King
millions of suns and moons and stars are
shining!

He is the Mind within my mind: He is the Eye
within mine eye.

Ah, could my mind and eyes be one! Could my
love but reach to my Lover! Could but the
fiery heat of my heart be cooled!

Kabir says: "When you unite love with the
Lover, then you have love's perfection."

XCIV

I. 92. *avadhū begam des hamārā*

O SADHU! my land is a sorrowless land.
I cry aloud to all, to the king and the beggar, the emperor and the fakir—
Whosoever seeks for shelter in the Highest, let all come and settle in my land!
Let the weary come and lay his burdens here!

So live here, my brother, that you may cross with ease to that other shore.
It is a land without earth or sky, without moon or stars;
For only the radiance of Truth shines in my Lord's Durbar.
Kabir says: " O beloved brother! naught is essential save Truth."

XCV

I. 109. *sāīn ke sangat sāsur āī*

I CAME with my Lord to my Lord's home:
but I lived not with Him and I tasted Him not, and my youth passed away like a dream.
On my wedding night my women-friends sang in chorus, and I was anointed with the unguents of pleasure and pain:

But when the ceremony was over, I left my Lord
    and came away, and my kinsman tried to
    console me upon the road.
Kabir says, " I shall go to my Lord's house with
    my love at my side; then shall I sound the
    trumpet of triumph!"

XCVI

I. 75. *samajh dekh man mīt piyarwā*

O FRIEND, dear heart of mine, think well!
    if you love indeed, then why do you sleep?
If you have found Him, then give yourself utterly,
    and take Him to you.
Why do you loose Him again and again?
If the deep sleep of rest has come to your eyes,
    why waste your time making the bed and
    arranging the pillows?
Kabir says: " I tell you the ways of love! Even
    though the head itself must be given, why
    should you weep over it?"

XCVII

II. 90. *sāhab ham men, sāhab tum men*

THE Lord is in me, the Lord is in you, as life
    is in every seed. O servant! put false
    pride away, and seek for Him within you.
A million suns are ablaze with light,

The sea of blue spreads in the sky,
The fever of life is stilled, and all stains are washed
        away; when I sit in the midst of that
        world.

Hark to the unstruck bells and drums! Take your
        delight in love!
Rains pour down without water, and the rivers
        are streams of light.
One Love it is that pervades the whole world,
        few there are who know it fully:
They are blind who hope to see it by the light of
        reason, that reason which is the cause of
        separation—
The House of Reason is very far away!

How blessed is Kabir, that amidst this great joy
        he sings within his own vessel.
It is the music of the meeting of soul with soul;
It is the music of the forgetting of sorrows;
It is the music that transcends all coming in and
        all going forth.

XCVIII

II. 98. *ṛitu phāgun niyaṛ ānī*

THE month of March draws near: ah, who
        will unite me to my Lover?
How shall I find words for the beauty of my Be-
        loved? For He is merged in all beauty.

His colour is in all the pictures of the world, and
 it bewitches the body and the mind.
Those who know this, know what is this unutter-
 able play of the Spring.
Kabir says: " Listen to me, brother! there are
 not many who have found this out.

XCIX

II. 111.   *Nārad, pyār so antar nāhī*

OH Narad! I know that my Lover cannot be
 far:
When my Lover wakes, I wake; when He sleeps,
 I sleep.
He is destroyed at the root who gives pain to my
 Beloved.
Where they sing His praise, there I live;
When He moves, I walk before Him: my heart
 yearns for my Beloved.
The infinite pilgrimage lies at His feet, a million
 devotees are seated there.
Kabir says: " The Lover Himself reveals the
 glory of true love."

C

II. 122.   *kōī prem kī peṅg jhulāo re*

HANG up the swing of love to-day!
 Hang the body and the mind between
 the arms of the Beloved, in the ecstacy of
 love's joy:

Bring the tearful streams of the rainy clouds to
your eyes, and cover your heart with the
shadow of darkness:
Bring your face nearer to His ear, and speak of
the deepest longings of your heart.
Kabir says: "Listen to me, brother! bring the
vision of the Beloved in your heart."